Five Steps to Beat Exam Stress

Anya Bensberg

Anya Bensberg BSc (LSE), MA (UCL), CELTA (Cantab),DipSpLD (Northampton), APC: Anya has taught and assessed many dyslexic children and adults throughout her career. She is currently Deputy Head (Academic) at St Edmund's School Canterbury in Kent. St Edmund's is an independent co-educational day and boarding school for ages 3 - 18.

Anya's contact details are aeb@stedmunds.org.uk

Table of Contents

How to use this book 5

Recognising and dealing with stress 7

Staying focused, mindful and calm 19

Effective revision and time management 31

Setting your goals and sticking to them....................57

Getting it right on exam day 61

How to use this book

The book has been designed for immediate use by students. However, from a practical point of view, teachers may find it useful to enlarge the worksheets to A4 size for facilitation of class or individual teaching.

The contents originated in response to student, parent and teacher needs and has been used successfully in the secondary and post-16 phases. I hope it will continue to evolve as students and their advocates work together in the process of exam preparation.

Recognising and dealing with stress

Quiz

Complete this quiz to see what stress symptoms you exhibit.

Before an important exam I…..	Tick if this applies to you
Find it difficult to sleep and lie awake worrying	
Feel guilty when I'm not working?	
Find it hard to concentrate	
Get frustrated easily?	
Get a dry mouth, heavy pounding or a fluttery feeling in the heart, sweaty hands, twitching or nausea?	
Grind my teeth?	
Feel irritable, tearful, moody or antisocial?	
Lose my appetite, go on binges or suffer from an upset stomach?	
Drop or break things frequently?	
Feel overwhelmed	

Reasons for stress

Stress can be a good thing but there are times in our lives when we feel particularly overwhelmed with tension. Feeling stressed usually results from a combination of factors. For example, if you are having problems out of school it will be harder to deal with problems arising from your studies with a clear head. Try to identify exactly what is making you feel anxious and you will then be able to tackle each issue individually.

Take a look at these common causes of stress resulting from study and decide how many (if any apply to you.

Reasons students become stressed on advanced courses	Tick if this applies to you
" I feel that I can't cope with the academic standards of this course."	
" The total demands of the range of courses I have taken on are too much."	
"As deadlines approach I feel overwhelmed by my workload."	
" I see other people doing well and I feel that I am not coping"	
" I am surrounded by students who are panicking and this makes me feel anxious"	
" I worry about the future. Will I get the grades I need? What will happen next year?"	

Effects of Stress

Stress and anxiety around learning, particularly exams, can create significant barriers to learning and performance. Research suggests that high levels of emotional distress are correlated to reduced academic performance. Stress can negatively affect many aspects of development, making students feel negative about themselves and school. Some anxiety is normal and can be helpful to stay mentally and physically alert. However, when someone experiences too much anxiety it can result in emotional or physical distress. Students experiencing extreme exam stress generally do less well in tests and exams than peers.

For some students testing situations create a sense of threat is they are experiencing exam stress. This sense of threat then disrupts attention and memory function. This has nothing to do with intellectual capabilities. Students who experience exam stress tend to be easily distracted during a test, experience difficulty with understanding relatively simple instructions, and have trouble organising or remembering information.

Making thoughts work for us

Realistic thinking is looking at all aspects of a situation (the positive, the negative and the neutral) before making conclusions. In other words, realistic thinking is taking a look at yourself, others, and the world in a balanced, fair way.

A: Recognising self talk

Our ability to talk to ourselves and to think in words is a part of the human consciousness. Self talk is what we say to ourselves without speaking out loud. It is how we think about events and about ourselves and has a major effect on our associated feelings. For example, when we think that something bad will happen – like failing a test – we feel stressed and anxious. But, if you think you can pass, you will feel calmer. It is important to pay attention to self talk because our thoughts have such a big impact on how we feel.

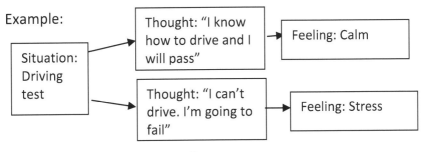

Example:

Situation: Driving test

Thought: "I know how to drive and I will pass" → Feeling: Calm

Thought: "I can't drive. I'm going to fail" → Feeling: Stress

Step B: Make self talk work for you

Listen to the voice in your head

- If you think, "I can't...", "Other people can...." or "I'm useless at...."etc
- Turn the message around: "I can....", "I have already....", "I am able to...." "I will...."

Question your way of thinking

Ask yourself questions such as
- Is there another way of thinking about this?
- Am I expecting too much of myself (or others) in the circumstances?
- Am I getting things out of proportion?
- What is the effect of me having this attitude?
- Am I blaming myself for things that can't be helped?
- What can I do to improve things?

It can be helpful to challenge your anxious thoughts because they can make you feel like something bad will definitely happen, even when it is unlikely.

Sometimes, anxiety is the result of falling into a thinking trap. Thinking traps are unfair or overly negative ways of seeing things.

Below are some examples of thinking traps.

Thinking trap	Example re: school performance	Realities
Fortune-telling: We predict that things will turn out badly.	*"I'll never pass English."*	*It is not possible can predict the future.*
Filtering: When we only pay attention to the bad things that happen, but ignore the good things.	*Thinking about the question you couldn't answer on the test, rather on the ones you could.*	*Make a list of positives and negatives. There are usually positives in any situation.*
Labelling: Sometimes we talk to ourselves in mean ways and use a single negative word to describe ourselves.	*"I'm stupid."* *"I'm a loser."*	*No human being can be summed up with one single word.*
Black-and-white thinking: Thinking only of possible outcomes at either extreme (really good or really bad) and not seeing all the possible outcomes in-between (or the "grey").	*"If I don't get a good mark, I'll fail."* *"I planned to study all week and I only studied for 3 days – I'm a total failure!"*	*Nobody is perfect. The bigger picture is how well you do on the whole course.*

Please turn over

Mind-reading: This happens when we believe that we know what others are thinking and we assume that they are thinking the worst of us.	*"Everyone knows I won't do well."* *"The teacher doesn't like me."*	*It is not possible to know what others are thinking.*
Over-generalization: Making sweeping judgments about ourselves (or others) based on a few experiences. These thoughts typically contain the words "always" and "never."	*"I always do badly in exams."*	*Just because something has happened once doesn't mean it will happen again*
Catastrophising: When we imagine that the worst possible thing is about to happen and predict that we won't be able to cope with the outcome.	*"If I don't get my grades I won't go to university and I will end up homeless"*	*It is possible to deal with most bad situations. Make a plan B for the worst case scenario.*

Thinking Traps feel true, especially if they are familiar. Perhaps you have told it to yourself thousands of times. The first step is to pay attention to what you are saying to yourself. It can be difficult to catch self talk because thoughts can come and go so freely.

Use these questions help challenge your negative thoughts or self-talk:

- Am I falling into a thinking trap (for example, catastrophising or mind-reading)?
- Have I been in this situation before? What happened?
- What is the evidence that this thought is true? What is the evidence that this thought is not true?
- What would I tell my friend if he/she was in this situation?
- Am I confusing a "possibility" with a "probability"? It may be possible, but is it likely?
- In one month how much would this matter? How about 5 years?
- What is the worst case scenario? If it did happen, what can I do to cope or handle it?
- Is this a hassle or a horror?

You now need to challenge your negative thinking by thinking helpful, comfortable thoughts.

For example, you have an important test tomorrow and have been feeling anxious about it. You think: "I'm going to fail the test tomorrow!"

To challenge this thought, you can ask yourself the following questions:

Am I falling into a thinking trap?
Am I basing this on the way I 'feel' instead of the 'facts'?
Am I sure that I will fail?
What is the worst that could happen?

Then use positive statements such as the ones below

- *I am stronger than I think.*
- *I can do this.*
- *I can feel anxious and still do it. I don't have to believe these anxious thoughts.*
- *Anxiety will not stop me from my dreams.*
- *I won't assume the worst.*

Worksheet: Stress symptoms and why they occur

Complete this quiz to see what stress symptoms you exhibit.

Before an important exam I…..	Tick if this applies to you
Find it difficult to sleep and lie awake worrying	
Feel guilty when I'm not working?	
Find it hard to concentrate	
Get frustrated easily?	
Get a dry mouth, heavy pounding or a fluttery feeling in the heart, sweaty hands, twitching or nausea?	
Grind my teeth?	
Feel irritable, tearful, moody or antisocial?	
Lose my appetite, go on binges or suffer from an upset stomach?	
Drop or break things frequently?	
Feel overwhelmed	

Stress can be a good motivator but there are times in our lives when we feel particularly overwhelmed with tension. Try to identify exactly what is making you feel anxious and you will then be able to tackle it.

Take a look at these common causes of stress resulting from study and decide which may apply to you.

Reasons students become stressed on advanced courses	Tick if this applies to you
" I feel that I can't cope with the academic standards of this course."	
" The total demands of the range of courses I have taken on are too much."	
"As deadlines approach I feel overwhelmed by my workload."	
" I see other people doing well and I feel that I am not coping"	
" I am surrounded by students who are panicking and this makes me feel anxious"	
" I worry about the future. Will I get the grades I need? What will happen next year?"	

Worksheet: Managing Thinking Traps

Realistic thinking is looking at all aspects of a situation (the positive, the negative and the neutral) before making conclusions. In other words, realistic thinking is taking a look at yourself, others, and the world in a balanced, fair way. This can be done by recognising self talk and then making self talk work for you.

Situation or trigger	Anxious thoughts	Realistic thoughts
Test tomorrow	I'm going to fail.	I will study tonight and try my best tomorrow. I passed the last test. I will probably pass even if I don't do that well on this test. I know I can do this

Staying focused, mindful and calm

Life can feel rushed at times. You may seem to be always in a hurry, lacking time and energy, with each day feeling like the last.

Higher levels of stress and depression are naturally felt by young people. Young people often feel under pressure to "do things perfectly". In today's society there are many new pressures – intense competition, real and online social encounters, internet temptations and a world of immediacy. The pressure on academic performance, body image and time management can seem all consuming. Various components of stress amplify each other. For example when we feel stress we tense up emotionally, leading us to become worry more about negative outcomes or possibilities. Furthermore, high levels of the body's natural stress hormone, cortisol, can lead to ill health and depression.

Many of the most successful, celebrated figures experienced significant failure before achieving eminence. Issac Newton was considered such a poor student it was thought best to simply let him run the family farm. He was such a bad farmer that his uncle had to take over. Newton then went on to Cambridge, where he flourished, becoming one of the greatest scholars of our time. Ralph Lauren worked as a junior clerk within a clothing retail company before conceptualising the idea of wider and brighter men's ties. He went on to sell 300,000 designs and start his own clothing brand.

In life, the greater success you seek, the bigger the obstacles to overcome. Yet for us all the following is true: you will never, in your life, ever have to deal with anything more than the next minute. However much you are approaching an event – an exam, an interview, an audition. If you mess it up life will not end. That will never happen. Minutes come one at a time and you will never, ever have to deal with more than the next 60 seconds. Just do the calm, right thing that needs to be done in that minute and if you can do one minute then you can do the next.

Ways to manage stress

1. Relax

Put some time aside each day just to enjoy yourself or to do nothing.

Try to get 20 minutes on your own in quiet. This is your time to take a break from all responsibilities and recharge your batteries.

Do something you enjoy every day. Make time for leisure activities that bring you joy, whether it be stargazing, a long bath with scented oils, playing the piano, or riding your bike.

Keep your sense of humour. Laugh at yourself if possible. Laughing helps the body fight stress.

2. Manage your time

Poor time management can cause a lot of stress. Avoid predictable crises and panics by planning in advance and getting started early to give yourself plenty of time.

Make lists, timetables and action plans. Use a wall planner to chart the run up to important dates.
Work out your priorities and when and how much time you need to do each task.

And finally, don't overextend yourself. Work out which things can wait.

3. Eat well

Eat fresh ingredients and plenty of fruit. Orange or grapefruit are said to be good for your immune system so can help with stress. Avoid excess sugar or caffeine. Does your body need more of substances to help it renew itself such as water?

4. Exercise

Sport helps your body produce endorphins, which make you feel good. Physical activity also gets rid of pent up energy. Walk, swim, run, play a game, clean the room, do some gardening. Chose to walk instead of catching the bus and take stairs instead of the lift.

5. Reward yourself

If you are working hard find time to take a break and treat yourself. Keep balance in your life by taking a day or evening off to meeting friends at the weekend. Make time to listen to music, go to the cinema or go shopping.

6. Stay relaxed

Try to sleep or at least lie in bed in the dark with your eyes closed and resting for seven hours each day.

When studying, make sure that you take regular breaks - at least once 5 minute break every 45 minutes. It will help productivity.

STOP! Stop everything for a minute. Breathe out slowly and count to 10. Smile and breathe back in. Let yourself be still. Repeat until you feel calm.

Mindfulness

It is easy to pay more attention to our own thoughts that the reality outside it, meaning we can get caught up in worries, anxiety, resentment and regret rather than what is happening in the immediate, real world.

Mindfulness is returning your attention, with acceptance, from your thoughts to your experience in that moment. Being mindful is paying attention to this moment in an alive and alert way and without distraction or judgement. Mindfulness focuses on this moment in time and what is happening within it rather than simply getting through it on autopilot. For example, stopping to notice your breathing, what you see, your movement, your feelings or what you can see, hear, taste or touch.

A mindful acceptance to a situation and to the feelings we have about it is taking a look with fresh eyes, and ignoring your habitual reactions. When we do this, we often see new, more useful choices. This may include accepting feelings that are hard to accept, such as stress and anxiety.

Start to notice what is around you. For example, by focusing on your own breathing. You may notice the breath against your nostrils or your chest gently rising and falling, how your body feels and any sounds or sights. If you are walking you may pay attention to the physical experience of walking.

It is not necessary to meditate for long periods of time, although you can. A good start is to simply build mindfulness into your day with some short and simple practices.

Try these 5 minute exercises

Eating – take a bite of your food and bring your attention to the sensations inside your mouth. Let the food remain in your mouth without chewing or swallowing. Then slowly begin to chew. Bring your attention to the flavour. Is it sweet, salty, rough or smooth? Try to slow your rate of chewing and control your urge to swallow.

Sitting – sit very still. Concentrate and notice the sounds around you. Are they loud or soft, gentle or jarring? What is your awareness – are these sounds recognisable? Can you hear birds singing, people chatting or fingers hitting a keyboard?

Observing feelings – Move your attention to the physical aspects of your feelings and observe your feelings as if you are curious about them, while breathing calmly. The feelings of stress should then subside, leaving you less likely to experience negative thinking.

Becoming mindful – 20 minute exercises.

Visualisation

This method uses your imagination and is a great for reducing stress. It works well at bed time.
 1. Sit or lie down in a comfortable position.
2. Imagine a pleasant, peaceful scene, such as a lush forest or a sandy beach. Picture yourself in this setting. If you have a thought, feeling or perception, see it as a bubble and let it rise up away from you and disappear. When it's gone, wait for the next one and repeat the process. Don't think about the contents of the bubble, just observe it. You should not allow yourself to be concerned by these thoughts, instead, just watch them pass over you.

3. Focus on the scene for a set amount of time (any amount of time you are comfortable with), then gradually return to the present

Muscle relaxation

This method is great for resting the body and making you feel refreshed. It works by helping you relax the major muscle groups in your body.

1. Lie down.
2. Begin with your facial muscles. Frown hard for 5-10 seconds and then relax all your muscles.
3. Work other facial muscles by scrunching your face up or knitting your eyebrows for 5- 10 seconds. Then release. You will feel a noticeable difference between the tense and relaxed muscles.
4. Move on to your jaw. Then, move on to other muscle groups – shoulders, arms, chest, legs, etc. – until you've tensed and relaxed each individual muscle group in your body

A mindful mindset

Mindfulness centres around being alert and awake, aware and responsive to what is happening within and around you at that moment. Developing a mindful mindset will encourage you to focus attention onto yourself. Through concentrating only on the sensations of the moment, mindfulness encourages us to find good in the difficult parts of life, even when life feels unmanageable, and to build resilience and strength.

Through providing space between your thoughts and your actions mindfulness will help you to understand your feelings and your expression of them. This, in turn, makes it easier to manage your emotions and your actions.

Below are a series of pointers to include within your mindfulness mindset

- Slow things down to help you recognise more of what is happening
- Allow your feelings to come and go; recognise each emotion
- Be aware of your interactions with yourself and others
- Observe and acknowledge your reactions and responses
- Be interested in yourself, consider carefully what makes you happy
- Breathe and be aware of how you breathe
- Be kind, gentle, honest and caring to yourself

Worksheet: Relaxation Checklist

Stress Management Strategy	Plan (or tick and/or date)
1. *Relax* Put some time aside each day just to enjoy yourself or to do nothing.	
2. *Manage your time.* Avoid predictable crises and panics by planning in advance and getting started early to give yourself plenty of time.	
3. *Eat well* Eat fresh ingredients and plenty of fruit. Drink plenty of water.	
4. *Exercise* Physical activity makes you feel good and gets rid of pent up energy.	
5. *Reward yourself* If you are working hard find time to take a break and treat yourself.	
6. *Stay relaxed* Try to sleep or at least lie in bed in the dark with your eyes closed and resting for seven hours each day.	

Worksheet: A mindful mindset

Highlight or tick the strategies you will try. Choose at least 3 from each section.

Practical behaviours	Basic organisation	Positivity and wellbeing
Declutter your life	Prepare for the morning the night before	Accept that you don't know all the answers
Smile	Schedule time for relaxation into each day	Look for a silver lining
Say something nice to someone	Be aware of each decision you make	Believe in yourself
Take a bubble bath	Always have a plan B	Visualise yourself winning
Stop saying negative things to yourself	Learn to meet your own needs	Develop your sense of humour
Ask a friend for a hug	Know your own limitations and let others know them too	Stop thinking tomorrow will be better than today
Stop a bad habit	Arrive early	Have goals for yourself
Practise breathing slowly	Have a support network of people, places and things	Look up at the stars
Learn to whistle a tune	Be prepared for rain	Hum a jingle

Please turn over

Read a poem	Set appointments ahead	Read a story curled up in bed
Watch a match and cheer loudly	Don't rely on your memory: write it down	Take time to smell the flowers
Do a brand new thing	Make duplicate keys	Work at being cheerful and optimistic
Do it today	Say "no" more often	Strive for excellence not perfection
Put safety first	Use your time wisely	Practice grace under pressure
Stand up and stretch	Make copies of important papers	Take responsibility for your own feelings
Talk less and listen more	Ask for help with jobs you dislike	Remember stress is an attitude
Avoid negative people	Break large tasks into bite size proportions	Set priorities in your life
Exercise every day	Anticipate your own needs	Look at problems as challenges

And lastly….. Remember to enjoy yourself!

Effective revision and time management

Many students find it difficult to get into the right frame of mind to study and often put it off. Distractions can include phone calls, social media, endless cups of coffee or snacks, TV, radio, browsing online etc

Prompt yourself to study

Many people need a prompt, or a set routine, to start studying. One student packs his bag and heads off to the local library. Another clears his desk before he starts studying: his prompt is a clear surface. Another switching on her computer, brings in a glass of water and opening her books. Some students might go for a walk to clear their head and order their thoughts before or after sitting down to study.

- Consider what thoughts or actions prompt you to start studying

- In what kind of environment are you most productive?

Tips to manage some common distractions

Distraction	Characteristics	Tips to tackle distraction
Lack of focus	Difficulty getting started and sustaining attention.	Ease yourself in by spending 5-10 minutes initially and then trying longer. Change your activity but do something that allows you to reflect on what you just studied. How would you use it in an assignment? You may find that you feel the urge to make some notes.
No routine	No place or set time to sit down and study	Establish a set place that is comfortable and convenient for you to work in. Consider what kind of task you do best first thing in the morning and late at night.
Friends	Phoning or texting friends	Ask friends to help you focus. They can ask you about the assignment or topic.
Restlessness	Wanting to do sport or go out shopping etc	Spend ten minutes reading your notes or a chapter and then give in to the distraction. It is possible to combine sport with a task such as going over material to see how much you remember

The image below is a small part of a bigger picture.

What is the picture of?

The part of a picture represents a lesson or your notes from a lesson.

Of course, you could use the picture to guess the rest but would have missed many important details. Similarly, you cannot fully understand the meaning of a lesson without referring to the bigger picture – provided by an overview of the course and the topics covered. Use the course syllabus of the contents page of a revision guide to obtain a topic overview for your course.

Once you have a list of topics you will be able to track how much of the course has been covered and how much you still need to work at. A course overview will help you to prioritise what needs to be revised. Start by making a list. Try to decide what is essential, what is important and what can be revisited.

While note taking, pay particular attention to subject specific words, theories, principles and procedures that need to be learnt, remembered and understood.

It can be helpful to think of preparing for a test or exam as training for a marathon. A runner training for a marathon trains regularly by practising for the event. You can also practise for the exam, by doing past papers. In this way you will become familiar with the requirements of the exam, including answering exam questions and working under timed conditions.

How to revise

Neurologists, brain specialists, believe that the brain is typically divided up into two hemispheres: right and left. The left side of the brain is for language and reading and the right is more creative and spatial. Put simply, some people have a preference for right or left brained learning – although it can be helpful to activate the whole brain when revising.

Learning Preferences

Complete the quiz below to see whether you have a learning preference

Learning statement	Tick if this applies to you
I remember people's faces but not their names	
Some of my favourite subjects are English, History and Languages	
You trust your gut instinct over everything else	
People have described you as perceptive	
Rules are important in order for society to function effectively	
There is a right and a wrong way to do things	
I am more artistic than technical	
I would read the instructions before assembling something	
I have difficulty expressing myself in words sometimes	
I am almost always punctual to appointments	

The italicised statements generally apply to a verbal, left brained learner and the statements which are not italicised characterise a visual, right brained learner.

Learning Preferences and Revision

Below is a table of proactive revision strategies that are characterised for right and left brain learners. Tick those you use already and circle those you will try to use in the future.

Verbal, left brained learner	Tick or Circle	Visual, right brained learner	Tick or Circle
Re-write notes using bullet points or make topic outlines		Convert notes into mindmaps	
Underline headings in colour		Make outlines or essay plans to organise your thoughts	
Highlight key words		Convert notes into cartoon strip pictures	
Use mnemonics and acrostics		Use colour and highlighting	
Read notes aloud		Convert notes into flow charts	
Get someone to test you		Write and draw images	
Teach a topic to someone else		Walk around while reciting or remembering information	
Listen to revision podcasts etc		Use interactive web programmes or videos	

Don't forget that some revision strategies work particularly well for some subjects. Mind maps can work well for theoretical subjects such as Religious Studies or History. There are many ways to revise and no one way suits all people or all subjects. Try things out and find works for you.

Revision Equipment

Get organised by making sure that you have enough of the following

Files
A4 loose-leaf files, leaver arch files or concertina files. Other key file equipment includes coloured file dividers and labels

Cards
Many students find boxed index cards, or other types of boxed cards work well for revision purposes

Notepads
Aim for at least one per subject. These can be used for keeping lists of key words and subject specific vocabulary

Highlighters
Practice using highlighters to add colour to your notes. Some students find highlight key words and command words on exam questions.

Post-it notes
Use post-it notes for last minute additions to revision notes. Post it notes can also be beneficial for any type of planning, since they enable sequences to be swapped around.

Planning your revision timetable

Getting the revision period right is key to the exam process. The exam is likely to be between one and three hours, yet it represents the opportunity to use the knowledge you have built up over several years. Balancing normal life with revision can be difficult but building a revision timetable will help you plan your time effectively. This is particularly important if you are given study leave before exams.

Start planning early. For example for A –level courses if you plan to spend two weeks revising each subject then this could require eight weeks of revision. Most exams start in May so the revision plan should be in place by March at the latest.

Below are some recommended steps when planning a revision timetable:

a) Firstly, make sure that you have all of your subject books , files and textbooks. Ideally, the books and files should be in good order with any stray pieces of paper filed away.

b) Make a list of the subjects you need to revise.

c) For each subject make a list of what needs to be done. It may be helpful to prioritise subjects, for example red for the ones that need the most time.

d) Plan your time. Make sure you know all important dates and times. Exam dates, your lesson timetable and any other key dates will need to go into your plan. You are not going to go completely without free time so build in some downtime such as time for meeting up with friends.

e) Then make a rough plan of what can be covered each day. Try to make sure each area of study is covered at least once. Ensure that sufficient blank time is left close to the exam for revisiting topics that require last minute attention.

Aim to stick to your plan as much as possible but accept that some days you may not be able to keep to it. Just transfer the session to an alternative time or the following week.

A well structured and comprehensive revision plan can formalise your revision but it is absolutely key is to have a list of topics and tasks to work through for each subject. You then need to get down to study and work through the list.

See overleaf for some examples of revision timetables and revision planning tools.

REVISION TIMETABLE BY SUBJECT AND TOPIC

Topics to revise	Time needed	Date planned	Comments

Standard Revision Timetable

Day	Early morning	Late morning	Early afternoon	Late afternoon	Evening
Monday					
Tuesday					
Wednesday					
Thursday					
Friday					
Saturday					
Sunday					

DAILY REVISION PLAN

WEEK:.................................

Mon.	....	
Tues.	....	
Wed.	....	
Thurs.	....	
Fri.	....	
Sat.	....	
Sun.	....	

Once you have your revision plan in place, remember that revision is a process of improvement. It is vital that you constantly re-assess how effectively you are working.

To chart your development you could try regularly attempting past papers for each subject. Mark them according to the relevant mark scheme and curriculum.

In addition, try the following tips

- Make sure you know the facts. When revising a topic, write yourself questions to test recall or understanding. After a break, or the following day, test yourself again
- Make plans for sample questions
- Explain the topic to someone else. Did they understand?
- Refer back to your class results. This allows you to establish a base from which, via further and regular assessment, you can judge your progress. If you have a bad result, make sure that you revise that topic again as you may need that information for the exam.
- Subject specific revision books, such as those printed by Letts or Longman can be extremely helpful revision tools, particularly if your notes are inadequate or you are struggling to understand.
- Ask for help from your teachers when necessary. Many teachers are happy to explain a tricky topic or mark a past paper for their students.
- Remember to check your revision timetable. Stick it onto your wall and keep referring back to it to see what is next. You will get a sense of achievement from crossing off subjects as you go.

Reading Strategies for Successful Revision

1. Reading Extended Texts: SQ3R

SQ3R is a reading method formed from its letters: survey, question, read, recite, review. Using SQ3R will help reduce the amount of time spent reading extended texts.

Before you read, survey the writing and look for
- the title, headings, and subheadings
- captions under pictures, charts, graphs or maps
- review questions
- introduction and conclusion

Question while you are surveying:
- Turn the title, headings, and/or subheadings into questions
- Read questions at the end of the chapters or after subheadings

Then ask yourself:
- "What did my teacher say about this?
- "What do I already know? What do I need to know?"
- Answer any questions

Reread the following
- Captions under pictures, graphs, etc.
- Underlined, italicized, bold printed words or phrases
- Read difficult passages again, reducing your speed
- Stop and reread parts which are not clear
- Read only a section at a time

Recite after you've read a section:
- Ask yourself questions about what you have just read, or summarise it aloud, in your own words
- Take notes, writing the information in your own words
- Underline or highlight important points you've just read

Reciting is important as you are using your senses to see, say and to hear the information.

Review

Once you can remember the information, you can start to review it.

- Reread. This is important if you are not confident that you've understood everything.
- Make notes if you have not already done this
- Discuss the material with someone else – this is an effective way to reviewing information. Explain it as comprehensively as you can, meaningfully and with examples.
- Review the information regularly to keep it fresh in your mind. Do this after a week, after a month, and after several months to allow the text to pass into your long-term memory.

2. BUG for Reading Exam Questions

BUG stands for Box, Underline and Glance Back. Some students struggle with understanding what exam questions are asking of them, especially under pressure. With mark schemes closely linked to question content it is vital not to misinterpret the examination question. BUG dissembles exam questions into their component parts, making it easier understand what is being asked by picking out what is required.

'Analyse how text A uses language to create meanings and representations

Procedural steps:

1. Puts a box around the word(s) which direct you on 'what to do' for the written task. In the above case the word "Analyse".

2. Ask yourself the question 'what' in conjunction with the boxed word. For this example: 'Analyse what?' The answer will help you to work out which are the key features. This leads to the underlining process.

3. The 'Glance Back' provides a self-checking strategy to make sure that words which are important to the task have not been overlooked.

Worksheet: What to revise

The image above is a small part of a bigger picture. What is the picture of?

What does this picture represent when compared to the larger one?

Complete the checklist below to get your revision started

I have the syllabus or topic outline for my course(s)

I know how much of the course has been covered

I have a list of topics to revise

I am using past papers

I am keeping notes on:

- Subjects specific words
- Theories
- Principles
- Procedures

Worksheet: How to revise

Complete the tick list below to see whether you have a learning preference

Learning statement	Tick if this applies to you
I remember people's faces but not their names	
Some of my favourite subjects are English, History and Languages	
You trust your gut instinct over everything else	
People have described you as perceptive	
Rules are important in order for society to function effectively	
There is a right and a wrong way to do things	
I am more artistic than technical	
I would read the instructions before assembling something	
I have difficulty expressing myself in words sometimes	
I am almost always punctual to appointments	

Below is a table of proactive revision strategies characterised for right and left brain learners.

Tick those you use already and circle those you will try to use in the future.

.

Verbal, left brained learner	Tick or Circle	Visual, right brained learner	Tick or Circle
Re-write notes using bullet points or make topic outlines		Convert notes into mindmaps	
Underline headings in colour		Make outlines or essay plans to organise your thoughts	
Highlight key words		Convert notes into cartoon strip pictures	
Use mnemonics and acrostics		Use colour and highlighting	
Read notes aloud		Convert notes into flow charts	
Get someone to test you		Write and draw images	
Teach a topic to someone else		Walk around while reciting or remembering information	
Listen to revision podcasts etc		Use interactive website programmes or revision videos	

Worksheet: Reading Strategies

Try BUG (Box, Underline and Glance Back) on the following past paper questions. Use this example to help you.

'Analyse how text A uses language to create meanings and representations

History
Describe Hitler's aims in his foreign policy

Physics
Suggest why the two lamps can have different power ratings but have the same light intensity output.

English Language
Write an opinion article in which you discuss the issues surrounding people changing their accents. Before writing your article you should state your intended audience.

Geography
Use a case study to describe how people use fold mountains

Design Technology
Explain in detail why the metal you have named in part (a)(i) is suitable for the luggage rack.

Biology
On islands in the Caribbean, there are almost 150 species of lizards belonging to the genus Anolis. Scientists believe that these species evolved from two species found on mainland USA. Explain how the Caribbean species could have evolved.

Please turn over

Business Studies

Explain why Noah's uncle believed that Noah's idea to form a company with limited liability would increase the level of risk for the uncle's firm.

Chemistry

Complete the diagram to show the arrangement of the outer shell electrons of the nitrogen and hydrogen atoms in ammonia.

English Language

Choose an event from Anil which you think is important. How does Noor present this event and its importance to the story?

Statistics

Sarah decides to stand outside a mobile phone shop one lunchtime and survey everyone who goes inside the shop. Describe one problem with this data selection method

Setting your goals and sticking to them

Motivation

Now it is time to examine your motivations for studying and set your goals. Motivation is the reason you act in a particular way or do something. In this case, the something is succeeding in your studies; this is your goal. Examining your goals can help guide the way you approach your study, as in the following examples.

Goal A: to achieve a good grade
If your chief priority is getting a good grade then it is important that you find out exactly what is required. Your exam syllabus, past papers and mark scheme will helps with this. Further motives to getting a good grade include greater satisfaction and eventually pay.

Goal B: to pass the course
Perhaps you should have switched after the first week but you didn't. Or maybe you have other demands on your time, or gaps in your education. More than half way through the course you may find that you need to limit yourself to covering essentials.

What is important is that once you are done you will have a qualification. You can then reevaluate what your options are and consider continuing your schooling in a different direction. For now, the focus is on finding and using the information to get through.

Goal C: You are interested in the subject
Being genuinely interested in something cannot be faked and is a surefire way to succeed. As Steve Jobs famously said, "the only way to do great work is to love what you do".

If learning about the subject is the most important learning outcome for you, then you may find yourself reading around the subject rather than following the curriculum. This can be useful for higher level study however be careful to cover all aspects of the exam syllabus.

Setting goals

By knowing what you want to achieve, you will know what you have to concentrate on and improve. Goal setting gives long-term vision and short-term motivation.

Goals are motivating when expressed positively e.g. "to achieve at least a B grade at French"

It is best to state goals in the present e.g. "I am able to follow my revision plan today"

Make goals achievable e.g. "I will pass my English exam"

For each goal, complete the table below

Goals: A step by step action plan		
My goal is....	*State goal in the present tense and using positive words*	*Use these questions to fine tune your goals* • Is it clear and specific? • Is it realistic? • Does it help me?
Likely gains		• Will I feel more positive about myself • Will I feel in control of my life? • Are there other possible advantages?
Possible losses		• Will I need to put everything else on hold? • Will I see less of family and friends? • What other sacrifices are involved?
Targets (short term goals – break into steps)	Step 1 Step 2 Step 3	• What things will I need to do to reach my goal? • Can I break my goal into small steps? • When are the best points to stop and reflect?

Goals: A step by step action plan		
Potential difficulties		• Who or what might try to stop you? • Have you set yourself too much to do? • Are there people who would suffer? • What other potential difficulties are there?
Steps to overcoming difficulties		• How will you overcome these difficulties? • Visualise yourself overcoming difficulties
How I will know when my goal has been accomplished		• How will I know I have achieved my goal? • What are my plans to celebrate?

Getting it right on exam day

An exam can be thought of as a performance. Every exams is a chance to use your knowledge. This is often knowledge that has been built up over several years and will be crafted into your responses to a series of questions. Pressure and nerves may make this seem like a daunting prospect but just remember that you are nearing the end of a long process. This, in itself, is an achievement.

The days leading up to your exams

If you have used the "effective revision and time management" section there is reason to feel upbeat about your upcoming exams. Keeping to your revision timetable and working though copies of past papers will help you avoid last minute nerves.

Make sure that you have studied at least one past paper for each subject and that you are able to answer the following questions

- How long does the exam last?
- How many pages are there?
- Is it divided into sections?
- How many questions are there in each section?
- Do some questions carry more marks than others?
- How much time do I have for each question?
- How many marks are there per minute?

Practising past papers is a key part of exam preparation. It is vital that you have some practice of answering questions under timed conditions. When planning your time in an exam you will need to take account of the time needed to reading through the paper and also to check it through towards the end of the exam.

The night before

Eat a well balanced meal.

Check that you have all the equipment you need and anything else such as tissues and a watch. You will not be allowed to take a phone into the exam room.

Check the day and time of your exam and also the room where it will be held.

Make sure that your transport arrangements are secure

Set your alarm so that you will wake up early to avoid having to rush through breakfast and getting ready.

Even if you have not finished all your revision, there is little point studying through the night on the eve of an exam.

Plan an early night so that you will get off to sleep quickly and wake refreshed. The few minutes before you switch off the light are an ideal time for memorisation. So once you are in bed, have a quick read through of the most important facts, equations or vocabulary. Then switch off.

On the day of the exam

This day is the culmination of many hours of study. Perhaps you are looking forward to the opportunity to show what you know. If you are feeling anxious it can help to ask yourself what is the worst thing that could happen should you fail. The reality is that student s are able to resit, repeat the year or take a year out to rethink their plans. Treat yourself positively, using positive language.

Have a balanced breakfast and before leaving home check that you have everything you might need such as Identity card, stationery etc. Then make your way to the exam in plenty of time. Avoid talking to other people on your way to the exam. You may start to feel that they know more than you do or have spent longer revising. Conversely, being around people who are panicking is also unhelpful. Any last minute revision should focus on mnemonics learned to remember key facts.

Go to the toilet before the exam starts, since exams can be long and there is no time to waste.

Breathe deeply and use the relaxation techniques outlined in "recognising and dealing with stress".

In the examination room

As you sit down at your desk, make sure that you are physically comfortable. You need to be able to concentrate. If, for example, you are sitting next to a hot radiator or your desk wobbles, tell the invigilator before exam begins. Also check that you can see a clock and the board showing the time that the exam finishes. During the exam do not be afraid to speak up if, for example, the invigilator's squeaky shoes are disturbing your concentration.

Don't worry what anyone else is doing. If anyone thinks you are trying to communicate with someone who isn't a teacher or invigilator you could get a penalty.

As soon as the exam has started, write down any information, such as mnemonics, which you have stored in your short term memory. This will reduce the demands on your memory during the exam.

Instructions

Listening to instructions given by exam invigilators and teachers will help you feel calm and well prepared for what is expected of you.

Reading the instructions on the exam paper is also important. These are usually at the beginning but there may be some at the start of each new section of the paper. Check how many questions you have to answer. Read the entire question paper before making a start. Often students will say they didn't check both sides of the paper, or didn't realise there was a question right at the back.
Fight the temptation to start writing the first question you come across on a topic which you have revised. Perhaps the wording is not as straightforward as that of some other questions on the paper.

Interpreting the question correctly

Make sure that you are clear on

- What the question is asking?
- What should be included in the answer?
- What the examiner is looking for in the answer?

It is tempting to alter a question to suit what you know or have revised. Avoid this by looking carefully at the key question words such as describe and explain and distinguish between them. Many students find it helpful to underline or highlight the key words on exam questions.

Read the questions very carefully and then, after a little consideration, select the questions you feel able to answer. Avoid questions that might reveal inadequate knowledge of the subject. There is no need to answer the questions in order.

Planning your time

Mentally plan when you will stop answering each question. Allow time at the end for checking.

Be careful not to spend too much time on your first answer, especially if you know a lot about it. You might run out of time for answering other questions and gaining those marks. It is a good idea to leave questions you are unsure about for the end.

Planning essay answers

You need to structure your answer and avoid wandering off into the subject. It can help to consider everything you know and quickly write down some notes. It can be a good idea to look for the command words in a question (words such as "describe", "explain", "analyse") and make little mind maps, flow charts or bullet point lists in your answer book. These rough workings can be crossed out later. Reread the question, crossing out anything you have written which is irrelevant. Then number the points in the order in which you will include them in your answer. Re-read the question to make sure you have covered all aspects within your plan.

In your opening paragraph explain your interpretation of the question. Your first sentence should rephrase the question in your own words. If the question requires short answers then mentally plan a concise sentence in your head before writing it down.

When concluding an essay answer summarise your response briefly at the end, referring back to the key words contained in the question. This helps convince the examiner that your answer has been relevant. Don't spend too long on this; a sentence or two is usually enough. Leave space between each answer so you can add anything you may have missed out.

Checking

Give yourself a chance to read things through once you have finished all your answers. Read through your answers twice paying attention the first time to meaning and the second to proofreading for spelling, punctuation and grammar. Make sure you have expressed your ideas as clearly as possible and that you haven't contradicted yourself. Once you are happy with your answers you should double check that you have entered all the information required on the front of the answer booklet.

What to do if the worst happens

a) You realise half way through answering a question that you have misinterpreted it.

If you have time start again and finish, if necessary in note form. If you do not have time to start again finish the answer you are writing as this will leave a better impression than stopping half way. You might not be penalised too heavily, especially if you included relevant information.
You can't answer the questions. Stay calm and take a deep breath. Remind yourself of the worst case scenario. You probably can answer one or two questions; they may just be worded awkwardly. Re-read the questions carefully. If you really cannot answer them see if you can answer part of a question to show your subject knowledge.

b) You run badly out of time
If you start to run out of time write down notes or a plan of the answer you would have written. You may get marks for this.
It may be worth checking the instructions on the front of the exam paper since students occasionally try to answer more questions than they need to.

b) You experience a total brain freeze

Take a deep breath and talk yourself through the panic. Think back to the room in which you had your lessons. Think back to the room in which you revised or visually how your notes looked. This will trigger some memories of your revision.

If all else fails, start writing – anything – and it is likely that you will remember more details.

c) You are unsure of some key information

It is possible that you will not remember a key word in an exam question that you must answer e.g. Being unsure of the meaning of the word "rogue" within an essay based question. If you must answer the question, rely on your gut instinct. Examiners are not out to trick you.

Afterwards

Finishing your exam is a great feeling but it can also feel strange. There may well be things you wish you had done slightly differently but everyone else will feel this way about how they did too. There is nothing you can do to influence them now and you are in the worst position to judge how well you performed. Avoid running through the exam questions with others. Instead, it is best to forget the exam you have just taken. Instead, use the time between exams wisely and keep your revision on track. If you have a little time between exams why not reward yourself by doing something frivolous – such as going shopping – before preparing for the next exam.

Examiners – the people who set and mark the papers- are looking for a good knowledge of the subject and a good impression. Remember – having negative thoughts is like going shopping with a list of what you are not going to buy!

Worksheet: THE DAY OF THE EXAM

My exam:

I know the following:

- How long the exam lasts
- How many pages there are
- Is it divided into sections?
- How many questions there are in each section
- The marks carried per question
- The time allocation for each question
- How many marks there are per minute

Checklist for the night before

Remember to do this	Tick when achieved
Eat a nutritious meal	
Check that you have all the equipment you need	
Check the time of your exam and also the venue	
Make sure that you have secure transport arrangements	
Set your alarm to wake up early	
Plan an early night.	

WORKSHEET: TEN TIPS FOR SUCCESS ON THE DAY

Tip 1
Expect the unexpected. Wake up early to leave plenty of time for your journey.

Tip 2
Before leaving home, check that you have everything that you will need – stationery, maths set, set text, map to the exam venue, etc.

Tip 3
Avoid people who are panicking. Tell yourself: It's going to be okay. Make sure you are mentally and physically ready before entering the exam hall.

Tip 4
Listen to and read the instructions carefully.

Tip 5
Read the questions through carefully and quickly plan how much time should be spent on each

Tip 6
Look at the key words in a question and then do a quick brain dump. You are allowed to do rough workings as long as you cross them out.

Tip 7
There is no need to answer questions in order. Remember to leave questions you are unsure of until the end.

Tip 8
Keep calm. If your brain freezes just start writing anything and you should remember more details. Remember to tell the invigilator if anything, for example a cold breeze, is distracting you. Remembers bathroom breaks are natural too.

Tip 9
Leave time at the end to read through. If possible read through twice, once for clarity of ideas and once for spelling, punctuation and grammar.

Tip 10
Don't dwell on the exam after it is finished. You did your best and you have nothing to fear.

Printed in Great Britain
by Amazon